Nocturne in Joy
Tatiana Johnson-Boria

Sundress Publications • Knoxville, TN

Book Editor: Erin Elizabeth Smith
Managing Editor: Tennison S. Black
Editorial Assistant: Kanika Lawton
Editorial Interns: Kenli Doss, Jen Gayda Gupta, Annie Fay Meitchik,
Robin LaMer Rahija, Lyra Thomas

Colophon: This book is set in Californian FB.

Cover Image: "Dusk" by Valerie Imparato

Cover Design: Kristen Ton

Book Design: Erin Elizabeth Smith

Nocturne in Joy
Tatiana Johnson-Boria

Acknowledgements

Thank you to the incredible editors and staff of the journals where the following poems were initially published:

Black Warrior Review: "Rapture: A Burning"
The Cincinnati Review: "Black Womxn Are Violets"
Foundry: "Ars Poetica"
Hoxie Gorge Review: "Here We Are in Infinite Joy," "Lucille Celebrates the Living," "'Since 2015: 48 Black Women Killed by Police. And Only 2 Charges'"
Hypertrophic, Fog Machine Press, and self-published in *for the love of black girls:* "Add Half & Half for Sweetness"
The Journal: "Origin of the Elements"
The Kenyon Review: "Before We Begin the Lowering"
New Delta Review: "Because We Were Poor and Unpretty" and "The Whales Chronicle Our Arrival"
PANK: "Heredity" and "My Brother Outruns"
Pleiades: "Triptych in Black & Blue"
Ploughshares: "My Mother and I Loiter"
Santa Clara Review: "Another Death"
Solstice Literary Magazine: "Awake in Elizabeth City," finalist for the 2020 Solstice Literary Poetry Prize
Southern Humanities Review: "Way of the World," selected as an honorable mention by Vievee Francis for the 2019 Auburn Witness Poetry Prize
Tinderbox Poetry Journal: "How to Make Love While the World is Burning"
Transition Magazine: "After Autumn"

Table of Contents

IV.

V.

For Black womxn*

*The use of "womxn" in this manuscript refers to women of any and all embodiments.

"There is no end
To what a living world
Will demand of you"
–Octavia Butler, *Parable of the Sower*

"I am not dead, but waiting"
–Audre Lorde, *Coal*

Heredity

My mother gives birth to apparitions
Her children exist in company of shadows

I learn not to be afraid of the dead
My father teaches how to exist among hauntings

In his prayers, he houses inherited pain
Expels his demons in his drinking

We watch our home crack open in séance
How our ancestors dance history alive

Our parents are vessels of antiquity
Rejoicing, mourning, reveling in our lineage

Trace these lines, they lead to ruptured paradise
Curious creatures swallowing a fullness of earth

In suspended portrait, a tree shields their bodies
Watch—my mother's mother give birth to ghosts

I.

Origin of the Elements

It is hot the day I am born
My father walks topless to the hospital
Sweltering, as I am born full of fire, humid
When he admits he has never wanted children
The truth is a scalding heat

My mother's womb is a cloud
That does not rain anymore
But once a miracle upon the drought
Of my father's skin, brought a tiny thing
He forgot to love

There was a time when the women
Threw their children into the sea
Salt pruning a new body old
Today the sea is a woman
With hands shaking from loving too hard

The tiny thing's first language:
Swimming—eyes wide curious
The earth sings the second language
Softly to the wind, landing on the tongue
Rancid taste of fear, never leaving the body

The water used to stretch for miles
Before my exit from air's blossom
My toes rooted in nothingness
Silent waves thick against ears
Vast Black clouds. The empty
Keeping me alive

My Brother Outruns a Dog on W. Concord St.

It is 1999. On the way home, the sidewalks sabotage our feet
with unequal bricks. Our legs drag from school, *straight home*
our mother says, every morning. It is the afternoon. The church
bells corral ladies to the sidewalk. God has a message every day.
They listen and mourn a man who died—rose. Each a version
of our grandmother. Cracked, Black skin, hidden under white gloves.
Cloaked knuckles clutching aluminum-covered fried chicken.
The smell floats past us hungry latch- key kids. So enthralled we
don't notice the dog. Panting. This dog, alive. The first one we've
ever seen. We are rooted. The dog, with a stare more confident than
all my nine years, my sister's seven. My brother, a restless wedge
between us. He is named after our father, but we call him something
else. We build a distance in the naming. My father believes my
brother is *just a boy.* My mother tells me he needs the pills to focus.
My father teaches the boy about fire. Hovers his small palms above
boiling water. My brother survives the heat. He is reborn unafraid.
My brother is darker than us all, no one calls him a curse aloud.
Instead, the recommendations are made. Enough to prune his unruly
edges. My brother has this look. The first time I see it, is after he
beats a boy who pushes our sister. My brother watches the stray,
with a look that reminds me that he knows how to protect. In this
stillness, he is almost foreign. Serious. His face placid against the
dog's howling. Our bodies still suspended. His body still and
unafraid. His legs churn. Sudden sprint. Past the dog, towards home.
His brown legs whisking beyond the dog's heaving. The bite
devastatingly close against a martyr in flight. Yet it all stops.
Fleeting as it began. The disinterested animal cowers down the
street, disappears. This beastly apparition, my brother barely
remembers. The speed of rising, a feeling, he'll never unlearn.

My Father Hums in the Kitchen
and for the First Time This is Art

Long before this, somewhere else, his father was killed
the memories are vague   my father's father is a ghost

We grew up with the absence   heard of some toiling man in the South
His hands a working thing   a without thinking thing

His voice a scream whispering from the back of his throat
His anger rising with sweat at the top of his skin

His pain crooning to the wind   a love that would dissolve
into nothing   to be passed down   except a disquiet melody
of a man against his will   to never cry

that faint sound steeped into   another son's body
who will then die   by the hands of someone else
cradling a   Black sorrow song in their hands

hands that wouldn't know   about his children   music blaring
through their gapped teeth   their feet pounding

to the origin of their father's atoms   A father who sighs
like he has a song caught in his chest   or cries   like a hymn

Way of the World
after Earth, Wind & Fire

On the day he is indicted
his oldest sister remembers
how he threw a rollerblade
at her face against their father
playing an Earth, Wind & Fire record—

That's the way, of the world

Her eye throbbing with each somber note
this memory now in harmony with her skin
her brother: just a boy. She young, unaware
the way hurt lasts longer
than the duration of a soul ballad,
wonders if her brother remembers
the origin of his rage?
Was it the aftermath of his piss-stained mattress?
The beating? The *pee the bed again and you're gonna get it?*

The softness of their father's records glides against a needle—

Looking back we've touched on sorrowful days

The sharp nature of a father with switch in hand
teaching lessons with his belt
The violence of his own father's death
drowned can after can, how drunk
that home must have been?
The memories a disfigured haze
still sleeping in some part of the body
lacing every bone of every child that lived there—

A child is born with a heart of gold

The boy, the first one, with the blade
named after his father, perhaps knows the most
of their fathers' demons. Finds his own over years
but as a boy:

> the fastest runner
> smiled Black joy while he chased down
> any kid who would step to his family
> wasn't the oldest but was
> a boy.

He and his oldest sister three moons
between them bound by rhythmic blood
the song on loop same anger in their veins
boiling different temperatures.
His simmering fentanyl. Hers mulling grief
of having survived the same house. Both
very much alive in what has
become a Black man's mausoleum—

Plant your flower and you grow a pearl

These descendants from anxious roots
remember the calls from their father
in other facilities, charged
with correcting.
Perhaps in what some
call a pipeline?
There is news
of an opioid crisis.
Remember that uncle?
A basketball star in the 80's?
Life interrupted
during another crisis?
When is there not a crisis
seething against a Black body?

Way of the world makes his heart so cold

This family ritual, melodic
a metronome beating with
every movement in their bones.
Their lives swallowed, buried
while the aria spins.
They do not sing.
They have forgotten
all the words.

Haibun In Which I Am a Failed Superstition

My father tells me not to split the pole. It is the only thing I remember because it is not literal. The meaning detaches from the physical, leaves abstract questions of how it could be possible to separate metal between my young hands. On the way to the playground, the bird's caw their existence, the path's agape with trees. Lush and wooden limbs breach. A brick walkway stretches through. We venture amidst the divide of branches. I am just learning to see beyond what is in front of me, this is my first metaphor. It is no surprise that I have never stopped believing how our bodies can determine the trajectory of what happens to those we love. The path shifts to concrete as a city bleeds through. My father guides me to never let a pole or tree exist between us. Each time we approach one meant to rupture, we don't let go. Instead, we shift our bodies for the purpose of staying intact. I absorb this practice as a balm for keeping the ones I love close. I wear this ritual for years; a charm for keeping lovers, blood and kin, anything—bound. I have grown weary of ceremony amassing in loss. My father's hands, runes of failing, collapse the world in his wake. How easy it is for my god's illusions to fade hollow. His frail sorcery kept mighty in my mind

> *the sparrows chanting*
> *psalms for which I must mutter*
> *spells of undoing.*

Because We Were Poor and Unpretty

After Gwendolyn Brooks

Our home haunted our clothes
Smoke dwelled in the thread
Made us cases in folders
In the office for the principal
For the social worker, for the
Teacher to understand, to *sigh*
To wish, to hope us somewhere
Different than how we arrived
Every morning, ravaging
Cartons of chocolate milk
For its rare sweetness in our
Brown bellies bloated with
Soup and bread slightly stale
Edible (on the weekends) from
The nice woman who smiles at us
With our empty bowls, winter jackets
Heavy on our backs at the shelter
My mother goes to alone
Some days while we are
Learning and forgetting
The house, our mother,
Her hands sifting
Cigarette after cigarette
Her lips breathing fog
In the evenings
The clouds dense
Her anxious lullabies
Crooning us to
Melancholy rest

Quiescent

We are breeding butterflies in freezer bags. In a plastic corner sits a vial filled with sugar water. Sweetness bleeds into the paper towel. Nestled inside they rest. It takes centuries (as a 10-year-old) to watch the hatching. The suspense is unbearable. I never grow out of impatience. *It's only 10 days* according to the teacher. I leave school each day. The apartment greets me with my mother's cigarettes. I bear it. My mother has stopped picking me up from school. She greets me from the couch. The ashtray is freshly used. Her body wrapped in the blanket. I have stopped wondering how long it might take for her to fully awaken. At any moment she will beam her teeth to tell me she is really alive. The house is quiet. I do not tell anyone I am waiting for something to be born. Yet, I dream about their entrance into the world. I wonder about the tenderness of their wings. What color awaits them. I am cyclical in the way I arrive at the classroom. Eyes guarding the Ziplock bags. I do not know how many days it takes before the rupturing begins. When the shell slowly breaks. The antennae stretch beyond the clear cavity. The body, clumsy. The flittering, halting. The burnt orange abdomen stretching. Normal miracle I've witnessed. I don't feel the entire class. The gasping of their young breath. When she says: *Their entire life can last as little as two weeks.* What kind of sinking was it? A future death? A stunted birth? I want to make something survive longer than it's supposed to. I know so little of this life. The definite space between the world and unknowing. I am the most helpless I'll ever be, still. How brief the world is upon arrival. How soon the ending of all things.

Portrait of a Mother Before Sunrise

My mother is Black
under the eyes in
twilight. Her mind
readies for midnight
ventures. The sleeping
hours have always been

her time away.
Us quiet children tucked
among the safety of night.
The hours, slow, and
swallowing, rock her
awake. Her feet
glide across the floor.
Our home resists the
pressure of her weight.

Her thinking begetting
unrest. How many
nights does she wait
for morning to yawn
into waking? Her eyes

open the entire time.
How heavy the body
rejecting rest fills
the lull of quiet. Fills
the worry to brim, stewing

slumber away—how all the
fear the body holds
endures in restless
weariness.

My Mother and I Loiter

on the front steps of
some young professional's
apartment in Boston.
           She smokes.
I hold my breath.
It is hard for both of us
to breathe.
Hers: heavy doses of meds.
Mine: small doses of meds
meant to make seeing her
less painful, other things
less crushing.
           Today it is hot
she tries to blow her cigarette
smoke away from me.
She doesn't know much
about me anymore
but she knows I've always
hated the smoke.
           She knows
I've always hated how we've
never been able to connect.

           She used to roll
my infant body in a stroller
while she fumbled through
schizophrenia.
           I knew nothing
but how to love her
the way babies know how.

The way babies don't
know that they
are experiencing

pain but that something
is breaking and my mother
is a hurting thing. But like a baby
she doesn't know this.
                So I sing to her
about my job and how the family is doing.
This calms her all the time.
                I imagine
she feels no pain if only for a moment
and I can smile as I wonder
if this is how it feels to be a mother.
                To know the world
and all its evil and to soothe anyway.
Even when the consoling never comes back
                and you're left empty.
I can't pretend to know about birthing
but I know how to make up happy stories
for a woman on a front stoop
who can't believe her daughter
is almost thirty.
                Who can't believe she had a baby once
chanting back every lullaby
meant to make things okay
meant to shield
                everything soft
like we are told
                only mothers could.
I don't know
                how to be a mother
but somehow
                I have learned
to keep
every hard
lesson tucked away
until enough time
has passed.
                Until the world
has aged us both

old enough
to learn.

Aubade Without Children

I am better here

with the doctors
guiding me away

from myself

with the quiet
begetting staleness

with my birds
grounded home

their pure sleep
unbothered

in cold static
a hallway

gives birth
to distance

Did they hear me when I left?

we fell in love
outside of this earth

our bodies
did the work

of swallowing

how we pushed and
pulled ourselves

into being
something else
into restless love

I am a stranger to this place

this is how we
learned motherhood

in this room
without windows

my body releases
the night

i am alone
they are alone

who will they be
when the sun comes up?

may they forget this departure
even if it means

I'm forgetting everything

may they still sing
with this mourning

II.

Nocturne in Joy

Today she is a pillar of sweat, the salt cleaves

her skin; the wife has not won the war, she looked back

to find the crumbling of her own bones. Her mother's

mouth, a memory, explains how when it rains while

the sun is shining— the devil must be beating his wife.

I can't help but imagine, supernatural warfare.

The wife: my mother incarnate, devastating vision—

The sky shows itself ablaze with violent clouds,

evidence of spirits in struggle. What are humans

but miraculous revivals of past energy

the world cannot dare to rupture? The endless existence

of our joys and failures. In the beginning, they are bodies

blameless in their being. The sky births them: in

beautiful aching, my descendants find their way to earth.

In beautiful aching, my descendants find their way to earth.

Some sort of love existing between downpour and daylight.

Smoldering a home alive with flood. A deluge of suffering

beckons each body to survive in ways only mortals can—

craters etched in skin. Marks of paradise birthing

parents. Sometimes a failed blessing is a family

wild in its restraint, harvesting phantoms. Children

dead and born again. Alive enough to know the coarse

edges of being young on this earth. An elder sings:

He's got the whole world in his hands. Recurrent song

a chant to remind us that we are held somehow

in the hands of someone eternal. The orb

of growing from innocence is carried infinitely, even

within the wounding nature of two humans in pain.

It is within the nature of a mother in pain to become something else.

My mother throws salt over her shoulder; becomes conjurer.

Each crystal falls in protection, a spell in the trembling.

Her hands in constant jitter, she struggles with being

partnered to beast. I watch her cradle a divinity beyond

us both. How we all grow strong from a mother's river

even when clouds fog the shores of her waves.

My mother inhales from a cigarette, the smoke

cradles her face. Alchemy in the finding

of peace, even in all its wrecking. Her lungs

cavernous echoes of her own breath. Midday

my mother sleeps to soothe herself. Her deep

exhales rhythmic, it is a miracle to imagine

her dreaming against the aching of our own house.

My mother dreams herself away from the chaos of her own house.

She does not sleep with him when he is home. Instead she finds silence

on the couch. A coven watches as my mother harbors us a home.

My father is a slurred song: *Bring me a cold one.* We children

do as we are told. We feed him all he'd like to drink.

His thirst riles his disposition to storm. He holds the rain

in his hands, my mother carries quenched fire in her palms.

My father gives me a choice: *Me or your mother.*

I learn dichotomy in opposites. I do not answer.

I wonder if my silence fulfills a prophecy of becoming

lukewarm in my needing. I bask in the tepid

weather I build for myself. This weather becomes normal.

I drift between a shifting tide like sailors do, except

I am too young to navigate the swelling surf of home.

Only on Sundays does our home swell with prayer.

My grandfather visits to anoint our stubborn heads.

He is Southern in the way he pronounces the letter "R."

This makes us laugh in the middle of his chants to god.

He teaches us respect by leaving welts on our skin.

It is a Southern thing to teach your children to fear—

the almighty finds a vessel in a man at a pulpit, the cave of his mouth

hollers stories of a man—I learn of for the first time

and again thereafter. It is His dying that makes

him memorable. I am asked to carry the death

of a son of a man inside of me. As if my chest blooms casket.

Who is a child but a carrier of the world she observes?

I eat the bread of a body to acknowledge he died for me.

I am already learning to be afraid of losing my existence.

I lose my existence in the gaze of my grandfather.

His eyes gleam discipline. They fracture our bodies

into growing against beatings. It is too soon

for me to realize fear as sorcery, as defiance.

How the story of the devil beating his wife

is parable. To caution the sun defying the presence of rain.

These are the things Black parents teach their children, to define

what no one explains. An incantation for violence in their own bodies—

the way the supernatural exists inside their ability to be soft

yet calloused in their loving. The collision of the gentle

and coarse leaves solace lacking in its soothing. Bittersweet

severity is the life of a child beholden to humans quarreling

against a swallowing world. A universe that begs

that labors in prayer, hands cloaked in oil, heavy with saving.

There was always enough work to cloak Nana heavy with labor.

She is no longer alive to show us the calloused portrait in her fingers

or tell us of her journey between the South and the North. How

land can transform breadth into density, foreign—

the way only migration can be. Even when the moving is prompted

by a loving she'd take years to cultivate, caring for it in all its

brutality— its calmness. How strange it is to have such extremes

growing in the body? Colliding with anything in its way.

Lineage is born in the midst of a rebellion of the elements.

My grandmother births a generation against abrasion.

Against the corrosive nature the world has against being Black and alive.

Her gap-toothed grin an heirloom etched upon her descendants

even in the midst of neglect a smile revolts, with the power of an ancestor.

It smiles gloriously through birth, through wreckage, blooming.

How glorious is the wreckage of a family leftover

after the ruins of joy—so raging it begets children?

And more children with fathers and mothers just as tethered

to the wounds of their parents. I am born in the gap of a damage

rotting itself into new healing. I was a child reckoning through

an ancestor's grief. I wade in an ancestor's joy. I forge a new earth

where a scar should be. It is birthright to know the anatomy of pain

birthing hollowed body human. Slowly learning to fill the breach

between what is and what can only exist as memory. The upheaval

of having lived through and through. How many lives have brought

me to one I am unsure how to take care of? I am cosmic ambivalence.

Flourishing uncertainty. A slight occurrence carrying

the weight of every reverberating echo of my blood.

Here, I carry the vast and difficult turmoil of someone else.

I watch my father pray against the turmoil of his own self.

He kneels his body against the edge of the bed, closes his eyes

asks for something celestial to protect him and his children.

It is in this moment, that the magic of prayer exposes itself

an irony. How all he has asked for lives in our home, assembles

around us, against the quaking of his own demands. Watching him

in prayer looks like a fallen angel at war with himself. He is part god,

yet holder of flames. Unholy contradiction. Blasphemous.

He's made a villain of being a man. Glorious are the survivors

of fraught roots. Building carriers of innate bitterness, fruit grows

amidst wavering harvest. I marvel the way my skin resurrects itself

where a scar once was. I marvel the way my skin remembers and forgets.

How wounds become ghosts, their presence known only to myself.

I am old enough to resist fear. I watch these spirits save me.

I am old enough to know that no man has ever come to save me

the way a woman has. I watch a Black woman fight death's desire

for her. My father shows me a film where I watch Black bodies

fall a pretend death. Based on billions of real deaths, and even on a

screen, I either watch us die or see a woman Black and stoic

absorbing it all. Brazen in her threat to be alive against death

or defiant in protection of her own life. I don't remember

how I learned to survive— if it was my grandmother surviving

her home, my mother surviving her own home or my will

to survive the home they birthed me through. I can't help but endure

being a body meant for carrying myself and everyone who never meant

to render their stories in me. Who am I to cleave myself from a narrative

larger than the lonely it brings me? A mere mortal formed of fragment.

I am small in a world begetting a collective survival.

I am small in a world that my family has revealed is a shelter

against the chaos of everything else. How is a home

a home when the turmoil lives on the inside? How is a home

a home when the turmoil brews against its shutters? I excavate

a home of myself. Carve my ribs hallowed retreat, contort

the insides into asylum. What kind of Creator am I? To gather

amidst ruin. What kind of God floods against me? I count

every ancestor weighing in and through me. I ask them

their names, yet their tongues are devoured by time.

They speak in the clamor of a fallen plate. In the wind

howling a window apart. They sit in my dreams. Quiet

yearning. They search for a vessel. They birth mourning

and praise. They are a heavenly terror I can't walk away from.

How miraculous is this epic between living and dying.

I am a glorious epic between birth and death. Temporary

survivor. What a privilege it is to wade this in between.

To carve the self sharp in enduring amidst all its learned.

I watch the sky break into oceanic flame. The burning sun

radiates against the rain. In the midst of hail,

the ground watches. Beholden to the mystery, the soil

can only absorb. The brimming heat, the soaking air.

The fog holds the world in stillness. Two gods

shatter themselves to harvest, yielding

this earth among the wreckage. When the sky opens

itself, the land becomes a body, speckling

a womb, a gateway. A universe yawns itself alive.

Imagine its Black mouth chanting, its own arrival.

Beloved to its own self, praise its blessed ascent.

To love your own self is to pray too for ascension. To carve

the self enormous, holy arch built from failures. Surrender

the self to mend, carrying severed limbs. Forge a future relief

rooted in a heavy too inescapable to not succumb.

Beneath its swooning, carry the glistening gap, the blasphemous

god you were born from. Shoulder the vastness lingering

between the ones who birthed you. Let the smolder of ash

your mother sweeps from her cigarettes seize you

in rapture. Watch them gleam inexorable

in your memory. These origins heaving

their pain. Even when you've attempted to cut away

your own belonging. Find yourself: extraneous stock. Pull

yourself from the turmoil of this ground. Rip the stubborn stalk

of who you are. Devour the sacred self abounding.

Today she is a pillar of sweat, the salt cleaves her skin.

In beautiful aching, my descendants find their way to earth.

It is within the nature of a mother in pain to become something else.

My mother dreams herself away from the chaos of her own house.

Only on Sundays does our home swell with prayer.

I lose my own existence in the gaze of my grandfather.

There was always enough work to cloak Nana heavy with labor.

How glorious is the wreckage of a family leftover.

I watch my father pray against the turmoil of his own self.

I am old enough to know that no man has ever come to save me.

I am small in a world that my family has revealed is a shelter.

I am a glorious epic between birth and death, temporary.

I love my own self, I pray for ascension. To carve—

To devour the sacred self abounding.

III.

Ars Poetica

A walk   through a field   carrying   my mother's wounds
The glorious   gap   in my grandmother's
teeth   The iron   swallowing
   the wrinkles   from my sister's dress   My stubborn
     brothers   throw their heads back   in laughter
I marvel   the harvest   of their uncombed
kinks   A phantom of a father   the tremor of his
voice   My mother   silent exorcist   *on a good day*
The roaches praising   the empty of the night
The oven open   it's yawn devours   the brittle cold
Winter unyielding   it wills   to break
My grandmother and her children   squatters in an   empty
brownstone   The passing down   of how to thaw   the absence
of money   We do not count   The lessons of   growing
up   without
Instead—
My great-aunt remembers   her mother   a master of
bearing joy   While cleaning others' homes   how ample humility
     runs in the caretaker
When she is forced   to forget everything   I watch her in a
facility   The quiet blink of her eyes   a drowning past
     she's unable to tell me   When she dies
I visit her home   the land   expands   a restless   root

She is buried   next to her husband

Who is buried   next to her daughter

Who is buried   next to her son

Who is not buried next to his nephew   who dies

Many years later   in utter silence   a memory

revives   an ancestor   Who unearths

    itself to marvel   the vast   and fertile   infinite

Awake in Elizabeth City

The air in North Carolina demands
you to breathe deep, a challenge
for the body to stall, the quickness
in its blood. There is no rushing here,

only time birthing more time.
There is abundance. A surmounting
wealth of space, begging you to see
it spread for miles. The dirt caves

in ditches in front of each home,
a crumbling net to catch the swelling
of rain against the flatness of earth.
Everything here is holding something

together. In a home there is a woman
who knows my mother's ghost, who
knows my grandmother's legacy.
She invites me in her arms because
this place holds anything that returns.

We don't know how many of those who
looked like us toiled the ground, mercantile
bondage beneath our feet. I imagine their

faces must soften to know their
seeds were delivered outside
confinement, amidst the restraint.

At my great grandmother's funeral,
the four walls of the church inhale,
with people who knew the woman,

who bore the woman, who bore me.
I know so little of lineage, yet I cannot
help but weep when I feel every spirit

howl against an organ. I watch a body
that used to sweat through her years
providing for her family nestled deep

in a casket, the same grind of
her living, stirs my bones into
building something out of some

thing someone else built for me.
How fortunate I am, to have

come from somewhere as
bountiful as this land, as

this woman, finally at rest.
When the doors break,

a flood of Black women
release in waves of lavish

hats, an elegant landscape
in their dresses, fanning

the onyx of their delicate
collarbones. When I am

released back into
the Southern sun

I am carried into
the arms of women

each with a different prayer
on her tongue, each twang

bellowing a different song
in all this harmony, I feel

nothing but tears pouring
from my body. In all this

drought, I am everything
buried roused to praise.

Another Death

The microwave whirrs   the hospital beef stew   to simmer

the air glides   through   the tube of my uncle's   breathing

machine   these breaths   monitored   his Black hands

pull the mask away   chapped lips sip stew   his breathing stops

for a second

between each bite   how much we are held   in suspense of his lungs.

He is the first son.   The only of his mother's children to die.

We do not know just how this   has happened   but here we are

caring for   a grandmother's dream.

In the beginning   a Black boy born in the 50s

a segregated image   before civic dreams

is a two-year-old on a beach   in North Carolina   dressed in a suit

by a   Black woman   who knew the importance

of looking   like you came from   somewhere good.

He did.

From two parents   who loved like sand   crumbling

against patent leather shoes.   From their friction   erupts

a Black family   who will buy a home   car   a slow anger

a joy   a religion   the belief that their

children will be fine.

Like most Americans.   Even when the years   prove

otherwise.   Even when   protecting your children

 is another form of faith   a hope

that is really just a home   on this same beach   disappearing

with each   rush of   the wave.

Until the only thing   left   is a photo   showing

he really did live   once.

His family was just   like any other blooming dogwood   just

like any other   Southern   ancestor   brought to the North

to live   to never return.   This is the story

of another way Black men die.

How time chips away   just as   much   life

as a brutal country   how cancer makes a home

in all of us   taking the years   the stories

as slaves   one by one.

Before We Begin the Lowering

We feel immortal
above the ground
walking among
willows grieving
the bodies withering.
The passing brings
us here, we can't help
but return when
the earth calls them,
we follow their
following of sound.
The ground
can't help but
cave to the weight
of our feet. It absorbs
the heavy above
while cradling
ancestors below.
My cousin's cousin,
(a small boy twice removed)
his crown of
tangled roots, his
knees sullied
with joyful falling;
swiftly brushes by me
his shrieks of joy startle
the cemetery's quiet
he runs between
gravestones unabashed
as the aunties reach
to shush him,
quelling his speed
to a stop. He is happy
with unknowing

we are sad with
having once known—
They're already dead
his voice: buoyant
echo, our faces soften
at the honesty
of this moment
at the grin growing
crescent on young
Black skin. We laugh
at the life existing
in his words.
The poplars stretch
above us. The wind
rattles through.

Still Life

Small feet travel bricks—the hydrant breaks
Water is vast in its journey across asphalt
Play happens when a city bends, imaginative
Joy lives in the wading of the young
Kinfolk cooling their skin in open flood
Coils of hair catch rain swallowing in thirst
The heat of summer leaves everyone alive
Smiling, smiling on this concrete beach
Aunties watch the children revel in their Blackness
They are saved by their eyes, pools protecting
When the sun subsides the street glistens absence
The water flows cracking concrete apart
Asphalt steams, tiny ghosts rise from the earth
Gentle possession, yearning for innocence

Elegy for Kamille "Cupcake" McKinney and Neveah Adams

they both return
the people grieve

they are found unlike
how they are remembered

beautiful, beautiful, beautiful

how the sun must have wept
the nights they were missing

how the earth caves barren
for their unreturning

beautiful, beautiful, beautiful

the sky wrings itself
the torrents rage in clouds

their smiles are gone.

weep   for the
promise of
their origin

weep   for the glint
they echo into
the dark

weep   for the grim
journey outside
of a womb

weep   for lost time

weep   for a belly
of cackles
resounding

Craft Talk: How to Write a Poem About Your Own Death

Greet the poem
Ask it to:
Turn on itself
to rebuke its inherent beauty

Set out to talk:
About the dying
There is nothing
romantic about
Black bodies
transmute to cold

Ask the poem:
Bleed, anew
Weep in cyan
Suspend crimson
Gather rage
Allow a ruin

Beg the poem:
To erupt
Become fuse
To burn, burn, sear
us into something
Worth this earth

Wrangle the poem:
Ask it to avenge
To bring
To hold this
White space
To reckon

Ask the poem:
How do gods grieve?

Oh, this Black
this glory
There is nothing
beautiful about
our death.

Rapture: A Burning

Here lies   the air   from which she was   taken.

Thin   grief-ridden oxygen.   Smoldered

yearning   the beauty that stood   amidst it.

   How often   has   the sky wept   for   how

earnest   a wrath

          there is   in search   for *her*   *us*   *them*?

How many names   are there   for gilded onyx

in body?   How many names

     for the rarity   that is   a Black womxn alive   or alive to

speak for themselves?   Each morning   I wake

 and the sun shines   its impossible light.   I beg it to break

instead.   I beg the ground to arrest   us awake.   I beg the

rain to flood us   toward reckoning.   I beg this earth

to capsize us.   There is not enough outrage   for all the

taking.   We have not been shaken   enough.

the air   from which she was taken.

grief-ridden oxygen.

Smoldered   beauty that stood

the sky   earnest wrath   in search

for *her* us   How many names

        for gilded onyx in body?

How many names for   a Black womxn alive   ?

      Each morning   the sun shines

impossible light.

I beg it to break   I beg the ground to arrest

I beg the rain   to flood

  this earth to capsize

      all the taking.   We have not been   enough.

taken.   grief

Smoldered   beauty

                    the sky
earnest

                    in search   for *her*

How many names

                    for gilded onyx in body?

  How many

                    Black womxn alive   ?

                            the sun

impossible

    to break

    I beg   I beg

                                        this earth

        enough.

Breonna, The Beautiful

Lungs stretch
Releasing miracle
Of another moment
Rejecting death
The home returns
As it was
Closes in the living
Panels protecting
Against the shrill air
Shelter envelopes
Heat brimming
Twilight waning
Cool air of the night
The static of quiet
The peace of hours
Where the bodies
Rest, awaiting sun
The day's a faded dream
You left behind
On the journey between
Today and tomorrow
Before the shattering
Before *Who is it?*
Who is it?
You
Heavenly hum
Among sheets
Who?

You rest.
You rest.
You rest.

For Breonna Taylor

"You Know How They Do Us"

She says it because
she already knows
I know the answer
The only answer
When Black pain
gasps
in the face
of the helper
when the helper
cannot envision
suffering as *real*
as happening in
front of them

You know how they do us
these vessels of Ours
these containers of
flesh, these—
somebody's children

You know how they do
You know how they do
This body of mine

The pain is not
truly a pain
the body not
truly a body
the feeling anchors:
The inside to ache

The doctors are told
you are
womxn.

Black in presence.
Before the reason for the visit
the reason is secondary.
No one says this. It is felt.
In the brusque.
The body is not
truly a body—
it is theory. It is challenge.
It is a truth dismantled.

It is a haven amid hoarded
remedy. It is a rebel
against tight lipped neglect.

A prayer clamoring a cave.
It is listless in the way
it must always fight.
A harrowing
collapsing of power
willful insistence.

You know how they do
You know how they do
This body of mine.

They've grown comfort
In how they do
how they do
This body of mine.

IV.

Pantoum: A Spell for Our Living

In which memory were you born?
Colossal—God of an ancestor's grieving
What dreams were whispered into your skin?
I wake, in fear of what might die with you

Colossal—God of an ancestor's grieving
May each moment offer survival
I wake, in fear of what might die with you
I hoard memories against a world's devouring

May each moment offer survival
A tender harbor—in hands, in mind
I hoard memories against a world's devouring
Offer incantation—refuge among the universe

A tender harbor—in hands, in mind
I carry a power of fierce guarding
Offer incantation—refuge among the universe
Guide this spell to find you

In each memory you are born

EMDR

Eye Movement Desensitization and Reprocessing is a psychotherapy that enables people to heal from the symptoms and emotional distress that are the result of disturbing life experiences. Repeated studies show that by using EMDR therapy people can experience the benefits of psychotherapy that once took years to make a difference. It is widely assumed that severe emotional pain requires a long time to heal. EMDR therapy shows that the mind can in fact heal from psychological trauma much as the body recovers from physical trauma. When you cut your hand, your body works to close the wound. If a foreign object or repeated injury irritates the wound, it festers and causes pain. Once the block is removed healing resumes. EMDR therapy demonstrates that a similar sequence of events occurs with mental processes. The brain's information processing system naturally moves toward mental health. If the system is blocked or imbalanced by the impact of a disturbing event, the emotional wound festers and can cause intense suffering. Once the block is removed, healing resumes. Using the detailed protocols and procedures learned in EMDR therapy training sessions, clinicians help clients activate their natural healing processes.

//

Once the block is removed healing resumes.

//

The first time
I start
medication
for depression
I imagine
a light thing
burying

//

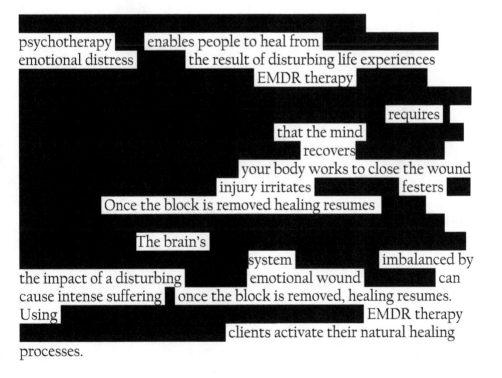

psychotherapy   enables people to heal from
emotional distress   the result of disturbing life experiences
                                    EMDR therapy

                                                    requires
                                    that the mind
                                    recovers
                        your body works to close the wound
                injury irritates   festers
        Once the block is removed healing resumes

                The brain's
                                system   imbalanced by
the impact of a disturbing   emotional wound   can
cause intense suffering   once the block is removed, healing resumes.
Using   EMDR therapy
                        clients activate their natural healing
processes.

//

I pull up my birth chart
for the seventh time
blame the neurosis on
my Mercury in Virgo
I pray to the planets
wonder about god
loving me
if I replace him
with stars
of my making

//

Once the block is removed healing resumes.

//

The house burns
On my father's tongue

It kindles his voice
A wrecking

The house is not a house
It is space next to
Space just the same

As any house for sections
Of the city both

Poor and unwhite

The rice is not white
Because I've scorched it to ash

//

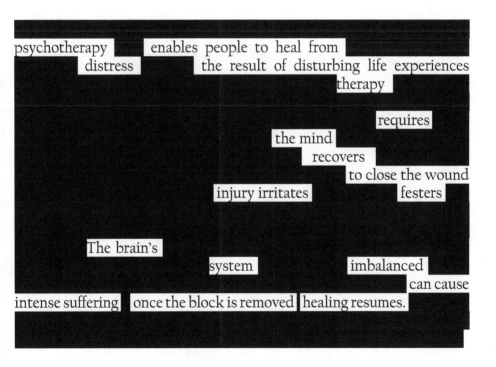

psychotherapy   enables people to heal from
        distress   the result of disturbing life experiences
                                        therapy

                                                requires
                        the mind
                        recovers
                                to close the wound
                injury irritates   festers

        The brain's
                        system   imbalanced
                                                can cause
intense suffering   once the block is removed   healing resumes.

//

My father stops
The burning
Before we all die

In the dead
Of night
I am learning
A lesson

The light
Of the stove
smolders
If left alone

//

Once the block is removed healing resumes. Once the block is removed healing resumes. Once the block is removed healing resumes. Once the block is removed healing resumes. Once the block is removed healing resumes. Once the block is removed healing resumes. Once the block is removed healing resumes. Once the block is removed healing resumes. Once the block is removed healing resumes. Once the block is removed *healing resumes. Once the block is removed healing resumes. Once the block is removed healing resumes. Once the block is removed healing resumes. Once the block is removed healing resumes. Once the block is removed healing resumes. Once the block is removed healing resumes. Once the block is removed healing resumes. Once the block is removed healing resumes.* Once the block is removed healing resumes. Once the block is removed *healing resumes. Once the block is removed healing resumes. Once the block is removed healing resumes. Once the block is removed healing resumes. Once the block is removed healing resumes. Once the block is removed healing resumes. Once the block is removed healing resumes.* Once the block is removed healing resumes. Once the block is removed healing resumes. Once the block is removed healing resumes. Once the block is removed healing resumes.

79

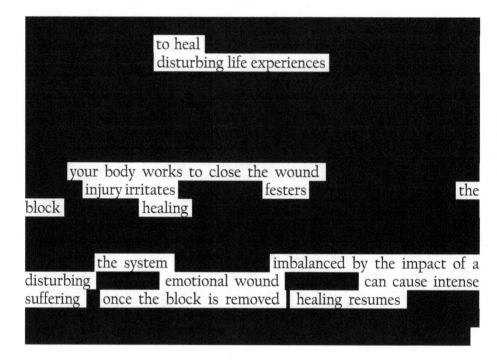

to heal
disturbing life experiences

your body works to close the wound
injury irritates   festers   the
block   healing

the system   imbalanced by the impact of a
disturbing   emotional wound   can cause intense
suffering   once the block is removed   healing resumes

//

On the medication
I carry the dark matter
Against luminous infinity
The nocturne beckons
My desire to live

//

Healing resumes once the block is removed.

//

White capsule
Moon swallowing dark
The universe reversed
Back into nothing

Or calloused fists beating
The house to cave
A rattle waking
The insides

Or the apparition
Of my mother having
Never left a ghost
Of her nurturing

//

The dead bolt locks us alone
the hearth of home sweltering
How we've grown to
sweat off the night

Or the closing in
Of the room
The bed—
All the bodies

//

I place gravity
On the wet earth
Of my tongue
Citalopram-slated
Beauty, swallows
This black

//

An eclipse happens
In my body, each
Morning, I am 10mg
Better than when I've
Awakened

//

I have not asked
This land to welcome
Me back, living
Is endless
In its mercy

//

The permanence
Of medicine, the faltering
Craters of me, the sun
O, the sun, journeys
The joy of my throat

How to Make Love While the World is Burning

I take my lover's face. In my palms. Ask my mind.
To swallow it. In the event. Someone yearns. To erase
him. I placate myself. A muted dream. Who can soar.
At a time like this? At the sex toy store. There is a
protest. The line of whiteness. Women with dyed hair.
Stopping the shoppers. I watch two Black women.
Interrupted and yet. They pass through. The door jingles
to greet. *Good for them.* I am asked not to cross the line.
I have been protesting for months. The vibrators await.
How much fight should I carry with me?
My sleep is deeper after an orgasm. I need the depth to
carry me. Away from being alive. At the end of a life.
I wake up to another death. One that is not mine.
I wonder about time. If it has as much hunger.
As violence does. I turn to my lover. They smile in their
sleep. I cradle into the gulf. Of their ribs, beckoning. Our
bodies wed. In the deep, I arch. Against the cove. Chests
rising. Their body, mine. Holy architecture.
How being human is an act of climbing.
The heavy earth. Of ourselves.
Into hands, glorious.

V.

The Whales Chronicle Our Arrival

I. That Night Was Silent Passage

Even the krill on our bodies rest silent. Dense
vessels moan across the Atlantic. We witness
the taking, the ocean heaves in revolt. Nomadic
ships carry carcels, wrestling a vast and endless sea.

II. What Drew Us, Like a Magnet to Your Dying?

How the plunge devours them whole. The bodies arrive
bound to flood, such tragic escape this journey brings.
The bodies float, in search of swelling release—
creatures of the depth release light.

III. Which Ancestor First Plunged Through Zones of Colored Twilight?

A mother's grief. A clearing scream. Hallowed eyes,
resurrected to bulge. A future death. A rooted wound.
Gravity flays buoyant existence, soaking skin back to bone.

IV. Scour the Bottom of the Dark

An ancestor lives on every acre of the deep.
Here, they gather wrangled gods. Here, they cherish the depth
of their skin. Here, they praise descendants of Cain.
Their song finds our echo, ripples sonic hymn.

V. You Have Become Gods in Exile

The ocean billows survival, a haunting psalm.
What scattered inheritance this sin bears.
How you've become us, endangered in the dark.
Marine-ridden and immortal, yielding holy flood.

After Autumn
for the girls at Orchard Gardens Middle School

It is too late at the orchard
for the fruit have already

fallen   bruised   juice
stilted   on the inside

A girl tells me she has
never heard a poem

about a Black   girl
but has heard poems
about   apples

I try to sketch her
as fruit   red   shining
optimism of   being alive

How pure it is to be
deathless   12-year-old
laugh filled   with glitter

like Jahi's   nails
who look   like Cardi's—

ten bejeweled   mosaic stems
rooted in a   Black Oakland girl
thought   to be dead

sweet sparkling from her
cornrows to   the tip of her
enduring fingers— It is Ruby

who reminds me at a young age
of how   it rarely matters
how small   unassuming

it is to walk to school
the world   will crush
your   belonging—

like Nia's cheeks   glimmering
gold   once   dew-soaked

her body   fallen
into the earth   gone

from safety's   branch
a thing   someone
thought   to slice—

This orchard   this fruit
a glorious   ebbing
from voice to   movement

born through Sandy
speaking   her life
into   fruition

How weary it is
to have arrived:
this   forgotten

harvest   visions of
the apples   breathing
before   a fall

Black Womxn are Violets

After Alice Dunbar Nelson

wild   wistful[1]
lovers   wander
the fields[2]

perfumed and deadening[3]
far from   sweet
clear perfect loneliness

god[4]   made
wild violets
heaven mounting
dreams

---

[1] in which the body once existed. in which the ashes swallowed breathing. in which something lived yearning for sound.

[2] expanse beckoning empty. folding itself into spell. protecting the ones forced into space, guided to rip the earth and self to ruin.

[3] in which there is always a palm covering the gaping blackness of a mouth.

[4] an origin, or ancestors, or root, or seed, or the uproot of it all.

Add Half & Half for Sweetness

A little girl
has told me
that I am Black
that my hair won't grow
too long and I believe
there is something wrong.

The woman whose hair
is as unruly as mine
says there is something wrong
when the cake is too dry
to always add creamer
to please the palate.

My hair is burning
in her kitchen
an iron close
hissing my scalp
the static of my hair
bakes knots smooth.

The woman who made
the woman who made
me dark and short and shy
in shadows, makes cake
with all the cream
in the kitchen.

The strands on my head
almost can reach, I *think*
my shoulders
this makes me feel more
girl and less Black thing
no braids

just straight dangling
beauty revolting
to curl back
above my ears.

And no one notices
the change
how sweet
I have become.

I stay away from the sun
the water
I sit inside instead
wishing away sweat
watching the Black boys
playing
their hair granite against the
wind of a jumpshot in heat,
hearts rising
with the rhythm of cake.

When the white hits
the batter
becomes something
more delicate
on the tongue.

Triptych in Black and Blue

After Carrie Mae Weems: Blue Black Boy, 1997

Directions: Make a selection from each column. Make a selection from each column. Make a selection from each column.

When no one has offered you anything Other than how to yearn for survival	You are born prism You are born dimension	Refraction glares holy Balanced against white
Scour the darkened depths Unravel your own lightness	You are born lustrous You are born mirror	Iridescent existence Echoing ancestor
Learn the axis of your skin By the cusp of your hands	You are born radiant You are born creator	The universe bends In curious reverence
Gather infinite realms To wait on your breath	You are born oracle You are born celestial	Guide this wild earth Kaleidoscopic hue
Orbit the unknown Gleam indispensable	You are born brilliance You are born indispensable	Stunning resistance Shimmering dissent
In an opaque world Beam your teeth	You are born defiant You are born God	Cerulean glimmer Most sacred of glares
A scream or smile With hallowed song	You are born alive You are born a marvel	Inverted beauty sings Mesmerizing hymns
You are born You are born You are born You are born You are born You are born	You are born You are born You are born You are born You are born You are born	You are born You are born You are born You are born You are born You are born

Self-Portrait in Excavation

Here lies the rich curve
of your grandfather's smile,
revel in its rareness, a bridge
from some ancestor's
laughter, how the buried
used to cackle this earth
into flames—there is sound
here in the darkness
you are steeped in,
some pain someone
passed onto you
because no one knows
otherwise and here lies
the aching of it all,
all the depth you long
not to traverse, all
the family you wish
would uproot but don't
you hear that song?
Billowing its Blackness
a joyful cloak? There
is no crying here or the
weeping does not exist
alone, you lonely thing
can't you see us smiling
can't you hear this sorrow
guiding you home?

"Since 2015: 48 Black Women Killed by the Police. And Only 2 Charges"

The New York Times, September 24th, 2020

I am the only Black woman
in the nail salon
I am here to become
a more compassionate
version of the self, I am
buried in
I revel in choosing a color
to gather my infinite
The bottle reads:
Hold Space
The woman *smiles* at me
guides me to the seat
I ready myself to place
my hands in hers
For the meticulous
shaping of fingers
For the refining
For the eroding of errors
The leeching polish
from months ago
claws itself visible
In moments she erases
the memory that
I have tried this
once before
Another day of grief
capsizing, the yearning
for vibrance colliding
with the depth
of my skin
My favorite thing
to tell a Black woman:

I love your nails
The light of her
face when someone
recognizes efforts
To care, amidst
a world's neglect
I do not remember learning
carefulness anywhere
else, I think
of my late uncle's girlfriends
The different women:
hair gelled atop
heads, heavy gold hoops
like my mother's—
SWV angels, their nails
O, their nails—
constellations rising

Lucille Celebrates the Living

Something has failed to kill the disquiet in bones. A celebration erupts from a corpse in dissent. Watch them smile in delight. Every tooth a result of someone's prayer. Starshine suckles the tongue. How the mouth carries hymn. The shaking of limbs rhythmic divine exorcism. Won't you witness séance in body? Won't you see the curve in our backs, the music gliding over? Won't you watch our thriving? Won't you carry us into song? By the world clawing away years of breath just because we were born. What kind of life leaves us unhaunted by our home. There are no parties where ghosts do not dance with us.

There are no parties where ghosts do not dance with us. What kind of life leaves us unhaunted by our home. By the world clawing away years of breath just because we were born. Won't you carry us into song? Won't you watch our thriving? Won't you see the curve in our backs, the music gliding over? Won't you witness séance in body? The shaking of limbs rhythmic divine exorcism. How the mouth carries hymn. Starshine suckles the tongue. Every tooth a result of someone's prayer. Watch them smile in delight. A celebration erupts from a corpse in dissent. Something has failed to kill the disquiet in bones.

Here We Are in Infinite Joy

*"People dance to say, I am alive and in my body.
I am Black alive and looking back at you."*
                    –Elizabeth Alexander, "The Trayvon Generation,"
                    The New Yorker

Here is the skin
the sun glares
its radiant
teeth towards

Here are the hips
mesmerized in rhythm
weighted blues, holy
strut, beautiful
as ever

Here they are
having cried through
some wrecking calm or chaos

Here they are dancing
for how could they not?

Here's how a song
emits the limbs
to swing

Are these words happy or sad?

Does it matter?
If the song
is a rich croon
in the body?

The knees arch
weathered joints
alive, with motion

The bass an arsenal
for euphoric convulsing

Here they are
Stunning celebration

How we move
How we move

Cadent glory
it is *never too much*
   never too much

Notes

The use of "womxn" in this manuscript is heavily inspired by my personal identity with some inspiration from the way the term is contextualized in Faylita Hicks' *Hoodwitch* and Aurielle Marie's *Gumbo Ya Ya.*

"Way of the World" uses lines from the song "That's the Way of the World" by Earth, Wind & Fire.

The title "Because We Were Poor and Unpretty" is inspired by the Gwendolyn Brooks' poem "Riot."

The first line of "Ars Poetica" is inspired from a line in "I Know the Name of the Desert" by Sara Borjas.

EMDR (Eye Movement Desensitization and Reprocessing) is a form of psychotherapy often used by those experiencing PTSD (Post-Traumatic Stress Disorder). This poem uses language from a medical explanation from the EMDR Institute.

"The Whales Chronicle Our Arrival" uses lines from Stanley Kunitz's "The Wellfleet Whale" reimagining the death of a whale to be in the perspective of whales watching humans die. This poem refers to the transatlantic slave trade, through which between 10-12 million enslaved Africans were brought to the Americas.

"After Autumn" is written for the middle school girls at Orchard Gardens Middle School in Roxbury, MA and Cardi B, Jahi McMath, Ruby Bridges, Nia Wilson, Sandra Bland, Breonna Taylor, Oluwatoyin Salau, Rekia Boyd, Korryn Gaines, Atatiana "Tay" Jefferson, Dominique Rem'mie Fells, Riah Milton, and each and every Black womxn not named here.

"Black Womxn Are Violets" uses words from Alice Dunbar Nelson's poem "Violets."

"Triptych in Black & Blue" is written after Carrie Mae Weems' "Blue Black Boy."

"Lucille Celebrates the Living" is inspired and dedicated to Lucille Clifton and her poem "won't you celebrate with me?"

Thank You

Thank you to the editors and staff at Sundress Publications who selected this manuscript for publication. Many thanks to Erin Elizabeth Smith and Tennison Black for your belief in my work. Thank you for giving this book a home and avenue to be shared with the world.

Thank you to the following writers whose work has, in short, changed my life. Kemi Alabi, Krista Franklin, and Aricka Foreman. Thank you for supporting this book and for being in community with me. Thank you Porsha Olayiwola for being my MFA buddy, a champion of my work, and, best of all, my friend.

Thank you Valerie Imparato for creating the incredible art piece for the cover of this book.

Many thanks to Emerson College's MFA in Creative Writing program where many of these poems were developed. Thank you to Rajiv Mohabir, my former thesis advisor, whose editing and care for my work heartened me to develop this book. Thank you to Dan Tobin, Richard Hoffman, and Pablo Medina for the classes that also inspired many of the poems in this book.

Thank you, John Skoyles. Thank you for believing in my work, your incredible insight, and for building one of the best poetry workshops I've ever been in. Thank you for your continued mentorship. You're truly an inspiration.

Thank you to the many wonderful writers who I've gotten the honor of connecting with at Emerson, in Boston, and elsewhere. Crystal Valentine, Princess Moon, Annie Zean Dunbar, Nehal Mubarak, Jaime Zuckerman, Rikki Angelides, Raina K. Puels, Livia Meneghin, Winelle Felix, Jess Rizkallah, Melissa Lozada-Oliva, Olivia Gatwood, and so many others not named here; thank you for reading and championing my work and encouraging me to keep going.

Thank you to the Southampton Writers Conference, Camille Rankine, and the many students in that workshop whose feedback helped these poems grow. Thank you to Jabari Asim, whose presence, wisdom, and kind words have motivated me to write. Thank you, Abigail Severance, my advisor at CalArts, who asked me the pivotal question: *Have you thought about getting an MFA in Creative Writing?* Thank you for your care and support of my artistry.

Thank you to the Writers' Room of Boston for giving me the space to continue developing this manuscript. Thank you to GrubStreet and the Boston Writers of Color Group for providing me a space to not only teach but learn from the incredible students I've met over the years. Thank you for all you do for writers, myself included. Thank you to Catapult for more opportunities to teach and learn from the writing of others.

Thank you to the staff and committees at the Brother Thoms Fellowship, the Mass Cultural Council, and the St. Botolph Club Foundation for the honors of receiving fellowships to shepherd this manuscript to the book it is today.

Thank you to my family and chosen family, who've come to every reading, shared every poem, and bought every book that my words have been in. Your support is invaluable.

Thank you to my partner Manuel. Thank you for opening a bottle of champagne to celebrate every acceptance, every fellowship, and every win (no matter how small). Thank you for your unwavering belief in me and, most of all, your infinite love.

And to my son Xolani, thank you for being a miracle without even knowing it. May this book remind you of the joy that forever awaits you.

About the Author

Tatiana Johnson-Boria (she/her) is an educator and expert facilitator who uses her writing practice to dismantle racism, reckon with trauma, and to cultivate healing. She's an award-winning writer who has received distinguished fellowships from Tin House, The Massachusetts Cultural Council, The MacDowell Residency, and others. Tatiana completed her MFA in Creative Writing at Emerson College and teaches at Emerson College, GrubStreet, Catapult, and others. Find her work in *Ploughshares*, *Kenyon Review*, and *Pleiades*, among others. She's represented by Lauren Scovel at Laura Gross Literary.

Other Sundress Titles

Age of Forgiveness
Caleb Curtiss
$16

Where My Umbilical is Buried
Amanda Galvan-Huynh
$16

In Stories We Thunder
V. Ruiz
$16

Slack Tongue City
Mackenzie Berry
$16

Sweetbitter
Stacey Balkun
$16

Cosmobiological
Jilly Dreadful
$20

Dad Jokes from Late in the Patriarchy
Amorak Huey
$16

What Nothing
Anna Meister
$16

Another Word for Hunger
Heather Bartlett
$16

Little Houses
Athena Nassar
$16

the Colored page
Matthew E. Henry
$16

Year of the Unicorn Kidz
jason b. Crawford
$16

Something Dark to Shine In
Inès Pujos
$16

Slaughter the One Bird
Kimberly Ann Priest
$16

The Valley
Esteban Rodriguez
$16

To Everything There Is
Donna Vorreyer
$16

Printed in the USA
CPSIA information can be obtained
at www.ICGtesting.com
LVHW011002221123
764639LV00030B/291